STARSTRUCK: Triangular Powers, Book 4 *of a series.*

Powers Above: Triangular Powers, Book 1

SUNBLOCK: Triangular Powers, Book 2

Do Not Swear by the Moon: Triangular Powers, Book 3 by Dr. Marlene

Miles Freshwater

Press, USA

ISBN: 978-1-960150-44-8

Paperback Version

Table of Contents

STARSTRUCK

Triangular Powers

Book 4

Freshwater

Freshwater Press, USA

Twinkle, Twinkle

When I consider your heavens, the work of your
fingers, the moon and the stars,
which you have set in place,
(Psalm 8:3)

In Psalm 147:4 the Bible tells us the number of the stars. He called them all by their names. How beautiful most of the Psalms are. They're poetic, majestic, even elegant, but then in the world we break it down to,

Twinkle, twinkle little star,

How I wonder what you are.

Up above the world, so high,

like a diamond in the sky.

Twinkle, twinkle little star, how I wonder What you are.

We will find out what a star is in this book--, not what gases and what's burning in a star, or how big it is, but the *spiritual significance* of a star.

Starstruck is Book 4 of a four-book series. Book 1 of the *Triangular Powers* Series is, **POWERS ABOVE**. The second book, **SUNBLOCK** spoke extensively about the types of people who use the sun to accomplish evil in the Earth, and what to do about it to protect yourself. The third book **Do Not Swear by the Moon** discusses the types who use the moon against other people, and how to defend yourself against that evil.

God has created the heavens and the Earth for our good, not to harm us. Now it's time we learn as much as we can, *spiritually* about the stars. This book is about stars in general, and about *your* star, in particular.

As in the first three books of this series, there are warfare and deliverance prayers at the end of this book, focusing on the *Triangular Powers* and deliverance for you and your star.

Recall, the *Triangular Powers* are the *powers above*, they are the sun, moon, and the stars. There are three bodies, the stars being collective, as one--, hence these powers are three, *triangular*. But I also say they are *Triangular Powers* because the agents employing these powers *triangulate* the powers.

God made the entire universe in Genesis. He made all the elements in the Heavens. He made the heavens to declare His glory. As we review, we are reminded that God lives in the 3rd Heaven.

Spiritually, we know almost nothing about *Triangular Powers* except maybe what we learned in 6th grade science about the solar system. The science teacher tried to teach us that we are in space, and where we are in space. A lot of people still don't know where we are. A lot of people don't care. But we need to know where we are, and who and declare *whose* we are. We need to know <u>why</u> we're here.

This is far more important than being entertained by a nursery rhyme--, *Twinkle, twinkle little star*. Its far more than twinkle, twinkle little star.

We are spirit, in bodies, on Earth. Jesus said that we can be where He is, so if we are in His realm, we need to understand spiritually, where that is. We need to know spiritually who we are while we're here. And of course, we need to know all about these *Triangular Powers,* especially the stars because there is evil under the sun. There is so much evil under the sun. There's evil on the Earth, because the heart of man is wicked.

The devil is wicked also, and he influences the heart of men to their basest nature, giving them permission to be evil and diabolical. He tricks some, but others are inherently wicked, so he *teaches* them.

Christians, if we don't do something about it, we'll be subject to some of this evil.
We pray to the Lord that we're not.

Satan is in the 2nd heaven, confirming that there *is* spiritual wickedness in high places.

For we wrestle not against flesh and blood, but against principalities, against powers, against the rulers of the darkness of this world, against spiritual wickedness in high places.
(Ephesians 6:12)

The *Triangular Powers* are three powerful lights that govern Earth and can affect humans positively or negatively. These celestial bodies were not designed to be weapons, but Satan has weaponized them and taught evil human agents how to do the same, to the degree that it suits Satan. I say that, because no matter what evil a wicked man dreams up, God won't help him fulfill evil. The devil sends demons to help a wicked man do wicked things, but only to the degree that it will benefit the devil.

For example, a wicked man might want to inconvenience his chosen enemy. The devil might want to *kill* that man's enemy. So, *without God*, what will happen will be what the **devil** wants because what man can *control* the demons that he has employed or called up from hell?

When something horrendous happens I've heard humans gasp, not knowing that anyone was listening, *It wasn't supposed to turn out like that!*

They lost control. Really, they never had control and were never going to have control over the devil.

Evil takes things to the max whenever it can so the outcome will always be worse, or the worst. The only time the magnitude of the evil won't be worse is if the evil human agent is sending death spells. Regarding killing, the evil human agent and the devil agree. Unless God intervenes, because the victim is praying, the devil may have his way. An unsaved person, a prayerless person--, the devil loves that. That's a two-fer, now the evil human agent is a murderer, and that person is going down--, spiritually and naturally.

Sorry, didn't mean to be so macabre.

The *Triangular Powers* could be why some of our prayers seem unanswered. It could be why our deliverance could be delayed or hindered. This could be why our lives need to be going better than they are. Wicked people using *Triangular Powers* is why easy stuff is hard for some. When there are ridiculous setbacks--, or worse things happening, we need to suspect *Triangular Powers. Triangular Powers* could be working against mankind in general or against certain *someone's,* in particular.

Night Skies

The good news regarding these *Triangular Powers,* is that as the sun rules the day, and the moon rules the night, God lets us know how awesome we are because we can ***command*** the sun, the moon, the Earth, and the stars; God has given us that authority. Amen.

So, in the night, when that relatively dim moonlight rules over great things, all kinds of evil may be afoot. We should not be afraid of the evil that walks in darkness, but we should be prepared.

Jesus said ***greater things*** we should do because He goes to the Father. Our Father and Jesus did **great things**. As we should be doing *greater* things, then that lesser light is ruling over greater things at night--, and that's us--, we are the *greater things*, also.

Created by God, a little lower than Elohim, we have been given authority to rule over all of God's creation.

This is not a joking matter, the sun is big and powerful, and it's a *smiter*, if we are not wise, naturally speaking. If we are not discerning, spiritually speaking, the sun is an afflicter.

If we believe only the moon, we will be convinced that the moon's light is enough, and that's all we need. In that scenario, that's as good as Satan and sin want it. If we walk only by the dim light of the moon instead of the brightness of the sun, and also Jesus Christ the SON, then Satan can run his game against mankind. It would be so much easier for the devil in that case.

In our proper positions and in our Godgiven place, we have authority over all of this smiting and affliction. In our proper positions and in our God-given place we could and should command the day because evil programming could be in the sun. We must command the day against evil and whatever has been put into the sun and other celestial bodies too. If we don't command the day, if we don't talk to the sun and the moon and command them, then evil entities and evil human agents will. And they'll end up using God's creation against us.

We pray that's not so.

We need to command the night. In the night is the moon, the stars, and a whole lot of mysteries. Evil man with his evil heart has devised or learned from wicked powers the way to use *Triangular Powers* against other men on the Earth.

Why would anybody weaponize a star, a planet, or the moon? Because man is inherently evil. Man is jealous. Man wants *things and stuff.* Man sometimes wants other people's *things and stuff* because the *things and stuff* that he has may not be enough for his greed.

In the temptations of Jesus, where the devil was saying he'd give Jesus this if He did this, and that, if He'd do that. **Jesus passed all of those temptations.**

The unregenerated man doesn't usually pass tests and temptations. The unregenerated, simple man wants *things and stuff.* And as I said, if there's not enough, he'll try to take *things and stuff* from other people. Hence all of this evil programming into *Triangular Powers* is to effect selfish and greedy outcomes of the carnal wishes of man.

I don't know if you're saved. I pray that you are. But if not, you may be thinking, well, *I'm a good person*. I'd never do **that**. OK, I'm not really talking about you, except to say that being naturally good is great. That should make your walking in your salvation, once you're saved, that much easier. But *good* does not equal saved.

A person could be naturally bad, but your own assessment of your being good is *your* assessment. We don't get to judge ourselves on this. God does, even if you are sin free. Sin-free Jesus said, **Why are you calling me good?** (Matthew 19:17). **There is nobody good but one, and that good one is God.** I'm just paraphrasing what Jesus said.

But if you will enter into life and keep the commandments.

You can't enter into life and keep the commandments if you're not saved. You can't just call yourself *good* just because you feel like you're following the Golden Rule or because for one reason or another do not have a guilty conscience.

God made the heavens and the Earth and everything in it. And then God said, **It is good. God gets to judge** *good*. God made us. God gets to judge. God is the righteous judge. God, who is

14

Good gets to judge. God says what's good and what's not good.

None of us will get into Heaven except we go by Jesus Christ. We need to go by that cross. Amen.

And you know, even with Jesus, some really bad people were born bad. Formerly bad people can get *in*.

And it's amazing, God's grace.

Bigger Than the Moon

The sun is a star. Every star that we see in the sky is each bigger than the moon. Look at the night skies. If you live in a very well-lit city, will be harder to see the stars. But surely, everybody's been camping or for a drive in the country where you can see how beautiful the stars are at night.

God told Abraham, He would make Abraham the Father of Many Nations, and your descendants will be as many as the stars in the sky. God said, **I'll make your descendants as numerous as the stars in the sky. God said that I will give them all these lands. And through your offspring, all nations of the Earth will be blessed**. Because of that promise and that covenant God made with Abraham, when it comes to the stars, I'd like to think of *us* as the stars.

- Any power that has struck my star or plans to strike my star, you be struck down now by God's war engines, in the Name of Jesus.

Joseph had that dream of the stars bowing down to him. Then Joseph's 10 older brothers took sibling rivalry and jealousy to a whole 'nother level. Then Joseph had another dream and he told it to his brothers.

Listen, he said. I had another dream and this time the sun and the moon and 11 stars were bowing down to me. NIV

Eleven stars--, that's how many brothers Joseph had. So, Joseph told his brothers about his dream. Joseph already had the favorite mother compared to the older brothers. And even if the parents treated all the kids the same, they had to see that Jacob favored Rachel over their mother, Leah, and of course, over the handmaidens. So there had to be some jealousy there, some animus.

It's very dangerous to be the favorite anywhere. Resentment probably had risen up in their hearts already and then Joseph had the nerve to have this dream where the stars were bowing to him. That was too much for the brothers, that's why they devised evil.

It's really dangerous if you're going to gloat, to be the favorite anywhere. You can be the favorite and not gloat. It's dangerous to be the favorite at work, at church, or at home, because other people will resent you, *eventually*.

For this hateful reason, Jacob's sons, Joseph's brothers had devised the scheme, which was in essence, to hijack or destroy Joseph's **star**.

Your star is really your destiny. In your star *is* your destiny, among other things, which we will share in this book.

These brothers may not have actually known what they were doing. They were just doing something that seemed that it would satisfy their jealousy and their flesh. Really, they were moving in blind witchcraft. These were not the nicest brothers to have; they took revenge to a whole 'nother level.

- Lord, keep my star safe from being struck by family, friends, colleagues, coeds, strangers, enemies, and fake friends, in the Name of Jesus.

This behavior of exchanging destinies ran in that family. Jacob exchanged (stole) Esau's star. Esau was the oldest; he had the birthright, but Jacob tricked him, stole it from him. This behavior ran in the family, at least in six of Jacob's older 10 boys. Four boys were of the handmaidens, so they didn't have that double dose of selfish greed as did the six, but they let their single dose take them into evil.

Laban tricked Jacob for 14 years. Generationally, the six older boys had trickery, thievery, and sneakiness flowing into them on both sides of their lineage.

Supplanter Jacob--, until his name was changed to Israel, behaved according to that name. This is why he tricked Esau. They had this trickery, jealousy and all of these sneaky stuff going on in both sides of the family. Jacob's mother had helped him dress up as Esau so he could steal the birthright from his twin brother, Esau.

Jealousy and greed, covetousness, all of that stuff, that's who wants **your** star.

Look at the successes of Jacob's boys who ended up making up the 12 tribes of Israel. But they were so jealous and drooling over Joseph's star and hating on Joseph that they couldn't even really recognize that they had it going on themselves.

Spilling the Tea

In your star is your destiny. In your star is your future. In your star is your education, your profession, your career, your marriage, your spouse--, the right spouse, your successes. Your ministry, your purpose, it's all in your star. Your star should not be exchanged and we're gonna talk about how this can happen.

Your star is bigger than the moon. Your star is part of the *Triangular Powers*. Your star has **power** in it. All the things listed in the paragraph above, and more are in your star. There is POWER in your star. When God gives a gift or a promise, there is POWER associated with the promise to cause the thing(s) that God has promised to come to pass. **Your star, which is bigger than the moon, has POWER.**

Your star should not be exchanged, lost, caged, buried, covered, hidden, or destroyed, although evil human agents do and/or attempt to do any and all of that. Your star should never be struck. And I'm using starstruck as a way of saying that the star has been struck. Not that as a person is starstruck, but we may mention that too.

All those beautiful stars in the sky will tell more of your business than your toddler who just learned to talk. They spill tea when they should be quiet. Else, there wouldn't be astrology, numerology--, all types of divination. God hates divination, but all those people who are divining are getting information from the stars.

They Want Your Star

Folks who are looking into stars, are looking to see if they want *your* powerful, glorious, destiny-studded star. It's easy for them if you're clueless and not doing anything **spirituallly** to protect your star. Protecting your star is protecting your destiny, your future, your marriage, career, education. A person who knows spiritually about stars, may launch an attack on your star to take it from you. They could exchange theirs for yours, or somebody else's for yours. People go to these diviners to ask for fame, money and other things that they don't have, shouldn't have, or should get from God. Diviners get paid by these greedy and/or desperate seekers. They do the stuff for money.

Divination will divide a nation.

This is why we must fight. This is the *why* of this spiritual warfare talk, because an evil entity may not really even *want* your star, they just may not want **you** to have it. They might want to get it and sell it to somebody else.

Warning, when a so-called friend tells you that they're jealous of you, they mean it. Conduct yourself accordingly. Sometimes they don't want your good success, they just don't want *you* to have it.

Did Reuben want Joseph's great star and the destiny that the Lord had revealed to Joseph in his dreams? The Bible doesn't really say that; he may not have wanted Joseph to have it. Just as sometimes a fretful kid doesn't want another kid's toy, they just don't want the other kid to have it.

People who invent things, know that sometimes a company will buy or license your invention, never to bring it to market. They just don't want it on the market competing with theirs. There's a lot of politics to this stuff.

Somebody might buy a website domain name that they never plan to use. They plan to sell it to you because they know the name of your company, so they bought it first to mark it up for a profit. People are jealous, greedy--, people want *things and stuff.*

On a whole different level and in a whole different way, evil will ***hunt*** a star. Your star. Any great star. That's why Herod in the New Testament was eyeballing that glorious star of Jesus. Herod or his evil people saw the star and told Herod about it, so Herod's mission became to find out whose star that was.

The Daystar

Jesus had an amazing star. When you were born, you got a star too. Sure, His was much more magnificent than ours, but we each have a star. When you finally get saved, your star is even more evident than it was before. In **your** star is your destiny in God. Your path to your destiny is better lit when the Daystar arises in your heart, and the devil hates that.

The Daystar arises in your life, when the power of Christ arises in you.

- Power of Christ that arises like the Daystar in my life, keep my star from being struck by star hunters, in the Name of Jesus. *Amen.*

Your star can be hunted, (Jeremiah 16:16).

- Lord, where satanic hunters have hunted me, hunters of God, locate me and set me free by force, by fire, in the Name of Jesus. *Amen.*

The only way an evil star hunter *cannot* capture your star is by the protection of God, because of His Mercy and Grace. Ask for that protection over your star.

Star Hunters

But when you or I step out from under covering we are at risk of the evil star hunters who are very patient. Their satanic patience pays off if we are prayerless, careless--, or sin.

Their intent is to ambush the children of God as we are going through our little wildernesses. If we're not walking upright before God, but instead sinning and roaming about in the wildernesses of life, going around and around, lost, complaining, wandering, in rebellion, confusion, idolatry, our star is easy to capture.

Idolatry is sin. It happened a lot in the wilderness. God hates idolatry.

Evil strategists study you. They study your situation, your future, then they run ahead of you to destroy your future and your destiny. How in the world can this happen? They're working hard every day, all the time to find out what's happening with your star and what's happening with you, or whatever glorious star they are after.

Too many Christians don't believe anything's happening, so they are doing nothing. They're just going about their entertainment life, yeah, I said that. Their relaxation and entertainment life.

Yeah, Christians, we have work to do. But then there's entertainment. So many people work just for entertainment, the pleasures of life. It's not for purpose, it's not for God, it's not for destiny. It's just for entertainment.

The spiritual part gets ignored. And that's how the enemy can get ahead of Christians who can get ambushed for not having done their spiritual work.

Why do I keep saying this? We look at the model of Jesus, who came to Earth for real purpose. Jesus wasn't here to do lunch with friends. Jesus was not on cruises other than in the boat to go across the Sea of Galilee to get to the other side. Jesus was the hardest working man in Ministry, calming storms, and whatnot.

Jesus wasn't just socializing, He was working. He wasn't just cruising. Jesus wasn't just walking around with His puppy to go sit and get a coffee. We're supposed to think like Jesus and have the mind of Christ. Why would we think that Jesus is the only person who came to Earth with something to do?

Adam and Eve were put here to work. Jesus came here to work. Why do we think our life is just supposed to be leisure? And we become angry when it's not. This is a big lie that the devil has put into the world. Why are we falling for it? It's a lie. **We have work to do.**

• Lord, I repent, in the Name of Jesus. Help us, Lord.

Star hunters are out there. They're vigilant, they're competent, they're patient, but Power belongs to God, (Psalm 62:11). Power belongs to God; but know that uncontested evil is powerful.

People who seek diviners are not necessarily walking in and saying, *I want a star, get me a star, or get me 1000 stars, and here's the money*. No, they are saying they want success, victory, fame, wealth, stardom. The diviner interprets that as the person paying wants a favor from a demon. Demons are described as spirit guides or people are lied to and told it is their deceased relative who will do this favor for their success. The diviner is the go-between. The favor from the demon costs the victim money. In order to make this thing that the victim wants, POWER must be involved. *Triangular Powers* comes to mind because of the level of "favor" the evil seeker is asking. There are billions of people who are not paying any attention to their star or praying to protect it. *Easy pickin's.*

Now the evil seeker may think this is hurting no one, but they are wrong.

Rise up, mighty warriors, and fight for your star. Fight for your future and your destiny.

- Every confidence of the enemy over my life, Break now, in Jesus' Name, *Amen.*

Your star is important. Again, what's in your star? Your future, your destiny, your education, your marriage, your spouse--, your real spouse, the right one. Your career, your children, your successes, your health and your wealth, your favor--, essentially YOUR LIFE! They're all in your star.

A star can be trapped. It can be shot at by evil archers like Joseph's was.

Archers attacked him savagely; they shot at him
and harassed him, but his bow remained taunt,
and his arms were strengthened by the hands of
the mighty God of Jacob. (Genesis 49:23-24)

Take comfort knowing that the God of
Joseph's father strengthened Joseph.

- May the God of your father, Jehovah
strengthen you and protect your star in Jesus'
Name. *Amen.*

Don't Give Your Star Away

Don't give up. Don't quit. Don't abandon your own star.

Depression, discouragement, ignorance and/or fear may hinder a person from realizing the value of their star in their lives. When a person refuses to **participate** in his own destiny, he is giving his star away. A person who refuses to participate in life, using his God-given gifts or ignoring his spiritual call from God, he's handing his destiny over to the enemy. Of course, there could be ancestral, foundational, generational interferences. For this reason we seek deliverance and stay prayed up.

StarStruck

Nobody wants a stalker. Not a celebrity, not a regular person, but if you star is twinkling, or chatting in such a way that it captures a star hunter's attention, and you're walking about the Earth unprotected, that is, with no spiritual covering--, then it's star hunting season. You could have just been born, as Jesus was, and evil was after Him.

You could be a grown person who doesn't believe in all that *stuff*. You could be a person who doesn't believe in God, or maybe you don't even know anything about God --, no one has made the introduction.

Maybe you *do* know God and believe you are saved, but you're prayerless and have no spiritual covering. Yup, star hunting will be easy when it comes to you. People see a glorious star and they become **Starstruck** – they want to be near mighty stars. They may want to be *with* that star, to *be* that star, or have that star. They need or want the power of that star to power some evil, illegal transaction.

In the Old Testament, Joseph's brothers attacked his star. The Midianites who sold Joseph into slavery (Egypt) attacked Joseph's star. Potiphar's wife attacked Joseph's star. More accurately, Joseph's brothers tried to **hide** or **bury** his star. The Midianites tried to **steal** and **sell** his star. Potiphar's wife tried to **demote** Joseph's star and **abuse** it. Here's some irony for you, the butler and the baker in the prison appreciated Joseph's star and honored it. Later, so did Potiphar. When people acknowledge who you are in the Lord and respect your giftings, callings and purpose, they honor your star. When they help you, they can be called *destiny helpers.*

In the New Testament, Herod was desperately seeking Baby Jesus to kill Him. Wise men from the East saw the star – *how*? They were star gazers, star hunters, though wise enough not to try to fiddle with that star, they came instead to worship. I consider the Three Wise Men as destiny helpers to Jesus in more ways than one.

First, they brought baby shower gifts that would last throughout His ministry and life. What they gave the child as gifts was pricey, but it may not have cost them a lot; we do not know their financial status. It may or may not have been a lot to them, it wasn't enumerated as a tenth of their holdings, but they were substantial gifts.

Furthermore, the Three Wise Men did not disclose the location of the owner of that amazing star that had put Herod the Great into great fear and a murderous rage.

In the Synoptic Gospels, all of the Jewish leadership agreed in their opposition to Jesus: the scribes, Pharisees, Herodians, chief priests, elders, and Sadducees EACH hated Jesus and they hated Him collectively. Did they hate Him as much as Joseph's brothers hated Joseph? Probably. Maybe more, but they were not able to lay hands on Jesus as many times as they plotted to and tried to.

And when they were departed, behold, the angel of the Lord appeareth to Joseph in a dream, saying, Arise, and take the young child and his mother, and flee into Egypt, and be thou there until I bring thee word: for Herod will seek the young child to destroy him. Matthew 2:13

At least eight times in the Gospels, people tried to seize Jesus and kill Him because of something He did or said. In the natural they seemed to be offended by Jesus' words or actions, but what if there was a deeper spiritual influence and the devil was using Phariseetypes to try to get rid of Jesus because of Jesus' destiny, because of His star?

Times when Jesus' star was unappreciated or under attack are many. If we recount how many times Jesus' human ancestors were attacked the count would be much higher, but that's for another book.

The devil's temptations of Jesus right after He had been baptized by John and driven into the Wilderness were all attempts to steal/exchange Jesus's power, I mean STAR.

Each temptation would have been a sin and sin opens a person up for demonic attack of all kinds including the striking of one's star.

Jesus could do no great works in His hometown because of their unbelief. Jesus said, *No prophet is accepted in his hometown.* Friends and family basically wanted to talk Jesus out of His calling and purpose. They drove Jesus out of town. They were attacking His destiny and His star whether they realized it or not.

They tried to throw Him off a cliff, but Jesus passed through the crowd and left.

At least two other times it is recounted in the Scriptures that the Pharisees began to plot how to **destroy** Jesus after He healed a man on the Sabbath, which violated one of their beloved man-made traditions. Jesus healed a withered hand on a Sabbath and also another time told a man to rise up and walk--, on the Sabbath. (John 5:1-18). The Pharisees wanted to kill Jesus and they told Jesus that He was breaking the laws of God.

For real? Can your neighbor come to your house and tell you what the rules of ___your___ house are? Of course not. Ludicrous—
Pharisees telling Jesus the rules of GOD.

Another attack on Jesus' star was when Jesus said, **Before Abraham was, I AM.** (John 8:57-58). When someone questions your spiritual identity, they are attacking your star. The Jews picked up stones to stone Jesus to death, but He just passed through the middle of the mob, and left. Now, look at Jesus' level of spiritual protection. YOU, ME, we may need that level of spiritual protection when we are under attack by people who are bent on evil and destruction. If we are under the scopes of people who know how to use the *Triangular Powers* and/or want to attack our star we could be in dangerous territory.

After many instances of Jesus doing good, the Pharisees decided that the only course of action left, to stay in power, was to kill Jesus, (John 11:53). See the relentless nature of those who attack stars and use *Triangular Powers?* If you don't have spiritual covering, you are especially vulnerable.

Ninety-nine-point-nine percent of the time they won't stop until they either consume you, or you stop them. Which outcome would you desire?

If the world hates you, you know that it hated Me before it hated you. (John 15:18)

People wanted to kill Jesus because they did not know God. When people oppose Christ and His way today, it is because they do not know God.

Star Down

Your star can be wounded. It can be captured, caged, stolen, or exchanged. Your star can become nomadic--, a wandering star. Bright and stable stars command great favor because your favor is in your star. In your star is your *divine connections.* In your star is your destiny helpers. Your star leads people to you just as the wise men were led to Jesus. Your star leads your right connections and your destiny helpers and your favor to you. If your star is gone, mispositioned, darkened or caged, people can't find you. And you may be asking, *How come nobody's helping me?* They can't find you if your star is not positioned and in its proper place, and shining.

You need to command your star to return to you, and to its proper position, if it's been lost. Your star can be cursed. It can be cursed by a person in authority over you, by your own words. Unfortunately, by some people's parents. We need to repent.

If we have spoken curse words over our life, over our star, over our destiny, and our future, we need to renounce those words spoken. We need to break curses, even if they were spoken by relatives, family, and /or so-called friends. We need to break those curses, by the Name of Jesus Christ, by the Blood of the Lamb. Amen.

A Billion Stars

Sometimes folks hate others for no apparent reason. The person does nothing to another, is not disrespectful, they may be super nice to another, but the hater just hates them. Perhaps the hater has sized this person up and resents that there is something great, something wonderful, something godly about this person and the demons in the hater just doesn't like it.

Based on His Gospel of love which a lot of passive Christians embrace right now, I'd say Jesus didn't do a lot of things to people to make them hate Him. Yes, He spoke truth and they certainly hated that. They still do. But Jesus preached forgiveness and love and was still hated. Marvel not if they hate you; they hated Me first.

Jesus could do no mighty works in His hometown because of their unbelief. You might see that in your family. Sometimes family members and household witches are the ones opposing your ministry. They say they want ministry, but they just don't want you to bring it. They want to choose whom God should choose to do the work of ministry. They say they are for peace, but really, they are for war.

Household witches, you can't stay hidden forever. God is watching.

There are at least a billion people worldwide who may never hear the Gospel before they die. How anyone who thinks they are a good person should try to limit who ministers the Gospel to a lost and dying world.
A BILLION PEOPLE may die never having heard the Gospel of Jesus Christ. I'm going to do my part, as should you. None of us should be trying to shut down anyone who is in God's plan.

Most of what I write and speak about is far deeper than Salvation. A part of what I do is to set captives free and also equip saints who all should be doing the work of ministry. It's how God wired me, and I will NOT apologize for it. Neither will I disobey the calling of God on my life, nor will I stand down. But you're a woman. Yup, and fiercely proud of it. There are Mary's and there are

Martha's. I'm a Mary. I look for Jesus in everything I do and everywhere I go. I look for Jesus in people I meet. If He's not there, let's see if we can bring Jesus into the conversation.

Star Jacked

Your star can be hidden, repositioned, caged. It can be caged by defilement, such as eating polluted food, dream food, or food dedicated to idols, you need to pray very well over your food in the natural, because as I said in the message, Defilement, we don't know who made that food or what their intent was or what they have spoken over that food.

You need to pray very well over. everything you eat and drink. Eating in the dream can defile you. Eating in the dream can cause your star to be caged. Stars can be lost.

You can be defiled by illegal sex in the natural and/or by sex in the dream.

When Joseph was in captivity in Potiphar's house as a servant didn't it appear that his star was lost, if you think about it? Potiphar's WIFE tried to defile Joseph. Uhhuh. Later on, Joseph went lower to prison. Seems his star may have been destroyed at that time--, **but God--,** the Mighty One of Jacob can restore us. We must pray.

So, the goal is that whatever happens to your star affects you. It affects your life and your successes and your destiny, your family, your marriage, your ministry, your bloodline, your health and your wealth. It affects it all.

I'll say too that what you do or *don't do* can also affect your star. If you're in the wilderness or wallowing in sin and become prayerless then that gives the enemy, that patient satanic star hunter, an opportunity to attack your star. Don't let your star become starstruck by the enemy. And especially not by somebody who is starstruck, who wants to be famous and rich and successful, and they're greedy and they want more and more and more. They want other people's stars don't let it be you or your star that gets stolen.

Just as Jesus' star was seen by people who recognized its importance, your life and your star should be significant for the people that you are called here to Minister to. Whatever God has called you to do, your star should be significant to them so they can find you. Amen.

I review that we don't worship the *Triangular Powers*. We don't worship the sun, the moon, or the stars. We don't worship ourselves, angels, people, or *things* or *stuff*. We only worship

God. The stars are not just up there for us to stargaze, although that can be very romantic and lovely. The heavens declare the glory of God, and the firmament shows his handiwork, (Psalm 19:1).

Stolen Stars

The *Triangular Powers* are there to give us heat and light, to divide the day from the night. God made them to demarcate the seasons and even affect the tides and the weather--, scientific stuff. The Stella Polaris is that one star that helps to keep the Earth on its proper axis. Very deep stuff.

Spiritually, we need to know what stars are there for. Your star is your future. *In a sense* your star is demarcating the seasons of your life as well. Your marriage, your education, your career, your successes in life, your destiny. It helps your destiny helpers find you. Your children are in your star. Your ministry. Your purpose. The future of your whole entire bloodline is written in the stars, as they say. The part in your bloodline where you play a part is in your star.

You can't afford for your star to be disrupted, stolen, caged, taken, covered, destroyed. You have to defend your star; it could change everything in your life and your children's life in your whole entire bloodline if your star is not in place.

What if Joseph hadn't fulfilled Destiny? What would have happened to his kids?

What if Jesus hadn't fulfilled His Destiny? What would have happened to all God's kids?

The stars are talkative. They give satanic operators a whole lot of information, including the person's destiny and their future. Diviners use what you might think is everyday stuff to pry information from the stars. They use evil mirrors, crystal balls, water in clay pots, water in a demonic basket.

Palm readers are looking at your star when they look at your hand. They especially like your left hand. Don't just give people your hand. Don't do it. And sometimes they'll touch you on your forehead like they're gonna pray for you.

They may be summoning up your star, your face by the river at night and there's your star just chatting. These are star worshippers, astrologers--, the horoscope people.

These people want to hear what's going on in your future to see if they want steal it--, oh please, it's not to help you. Although an innocent may be going to a diviner for entertainment or help. That's not what you're going to get.

Diviners and most often the people who frequent them want power. They want success. Things, stuff, fame, riches. And you know what? Maybe this is why celebrities are called stars, because they've got a whole lot of good destiny working for them, *huh*?

Evil Human Agents

There are a lot of wicked evil enemies out here. Evil human agents will catch people who don't watch and pray. We need to make sure that it's not us. We need to stay prayed up. To the negative the sun can smite and burn. It doesn't just rule over the day. The moon can rule over the night, and it can smite if evil is programmed into it. The term, *smite* refers to a pounding or constant, regular or cyclical attack. That means when the sun rises if you've done nothing to counter it, whatever is programmed into it will bombard you. Same for the moon. Over and over again until you do something spiritually, GODLY about it. Trying to fight evil with evil will never work, it will make things worse.

Have you ever noticed that superhero movies have one villain and one good guy, not two villains fighting each other, (usually).

That's life. A demon won't usually fight another demon to make *your* life easier, so you need God to overcome evil, not more evil.

When abused, the *Triangular Powers can program* sickness into people. They can bring evil against mankind. They can block destinies, marriages, and wealth because they're blocking stars and all that good is in **your** star. The light of the sun can be programmed to bring mishaps or disaster. If you notice defeat at the edge of a breakthrough, somebody might have your star, especially if you are in a dry season (prayerless).

Occultic people use *Triangular Powers* to keep people away from God, to make them live a random, purposeless, worthless life. They're star stealers, star hijackers, star hiders, star coverers star exchangers. This may sound really wild, but if you have been going through life just fine until **something** changed. You don't really know what changed, but something changed. You hardly noticed it at the time, but something changed. You might not know exactly when, but something changed. You used to walk in divine favor and your steps were covered with butter.

Where's the favor of God on your life now? Your favor is in your star. Somebody may have your star.

A person using *Triangular Powers* against you, unopposed can bring a lot of havoc. We must oppose evil programming by prayer.

Those who deal with the sun are super confident. Those who deal with the moon are also confident with they're quietly cool and deceptive, calm, and collected.

That's Mine

Most often occultic people are hidden and dangerous, especially if unopposed.

Have you noticed that some kid maybe, that you went to school with, who didn't do well on exams--, maybe they didn't even half come to school, but now they're out in the world and they are *everything?* You did very well in your studies, you may have aced everything in school, but in life you're just getting by. Your star could have been **exchanged**. You need to pray and ask God.

I'm admonishing all slack Christians, my slack friends, brothers and sisters to command the day, command the night, the sun, the moon--, even the Earth. Pray against evil exchange, even if it hasn't happened to you, it will not hurt you to pray against it. If it has happened to you, God will not only correct the matter, but you can feel by the Spirit, in your spirit when there has been a release. You can feel when something leaves or changes. As you pray more, you will know God heard you and answered your prayers. Command the days and nights daily, nightly, forever.

Pray for your star to be released until the Lord/the Holy Spirit indicates in whatever way He speaks to you; in whatever way you hear
Him that it's okay to stop praying about it. These are not one and done prayers. Fighting entities and evil human agents who use the *Triangular Powers* is usually not quick. Dr. D.K. Olukoya says in his book on deliverance from *Triangular Powers* that you will not fight this enemy in a hurry.

God is in us if we are saved. The Greater One is in us. Evil star hunters are not stupid, they are evil, even though they probably don't think they are evil. They think they are either wiser and more powerful than everyone else, or this is what it takes. It may be what it takes in the world in which they live. But unless you are a sinner, you should NOT be living in *that* world.

Before a diviner does anything against you, they may check for you and find that you're in God, you are Spirit-filled. You are a workman, studying to show yourself approved. You are a prayer warrior. You're not slack in the things of God. That diviner might just reconsider and not bother you.

Don't get this wrong, evil is insistent and persistent, insisting on its own way. Evil is destructive--, *by any means necessary*, and has three modes: steal, kill, and destroy.

Herod, for example, went through the country and had every child who might even be Jesus killed. You see how serious this is?

When somebody evil wants your star, they are not playing with you; they're dangerous. If they want your star or some other virtue that God has given you, this is no time to be doing nothing or to be at leisure.

Woe to those who are at ease in Zion.

You need to pray a hedge of protection, a wall of fire, a mountain of fire, around you by the Holy Spirit that is so strong that they can't even penetrate it. The Name of the Lord is a strong tower, the Righteous run in to it, and they are safe.

Woke Up Sick

Witchcraft that is woven into *Triangular Powers* can make a person suddenly sick, among other things. I hear numerous stories all year long about people saying they woke up sick. I hear it all the time and have heard it for years. I can't say I really understand it, but we stay prayed up because of evil programming into these celestial bodies causes those sudden attacks that hit mankind.

Because man is subject to attack in the night while he's asleep, you'd better pray for real. *Now I lay me down to sleep is not enough-*, it's on par with *Twinkle, twinkle little star* – child's ditties. Occultic powers program failure to beat depression, any number of evil manifestations into a person's life unless you are covered by the Blood of the Lamb and covered in prayer. Amen.

Spiritual Problems

God put you on Earth as something amazing, destined for good successes. We're filled with purpose. Just as you want good successes for your children, God wants it more for you--, for us. We need to be vigilant so when something *different* happens in our life, we need to ask God about it right away.

Pray first; life is spiritual. Don't waste time dealing with all the natural stuff until you know that it is a natural problem by ruling out the spiritual problem. Prevent these types of problems in your life. Command the day and night, among other prayers. These are not the only prayers you pray but do get ahead of the evil incantations and the evil programming. Real hunters go ahead of what they are hunting to ambush them. We do not want to be prey, so PRAY. Amen.

Evil is not stronger than good, unless we Christians aren't doing anything. Enchanters are up all night chanting, muttering spells, enchantments against their would-be victims, programming the sun or the moon, or the sun *and* the moon and the stars, hunting, trapping, exchanging, caging, destroying, selling off stars. It's their occupation, they are determined.

Christians, wake up. Witchcraft is powerful, unopposed; we must oppose it.

If the fire hydrant in your neighborhood was pouring out water, flooding the street, and you've got the tools to shut it off, but you do nothing. That's the same as not praying.

When virtue, goodness, success, and destiny is hemorrhaging out of your life, and out of your kid's future and all you gotta do is pray, then PRAY!

Start somewhere. You may say you don't know how to pray. Pray the Word of God. Find a prayer to pray. There are Extended Warfare Prayers in the back of this book and in the back of every book in this series. This will give you great prayer points to pray against *Triangular Powers*.

If all these things mentioned so far in this book are happening to you, war has been declared on you, whether you realize it or not.

Wake up, mighty men of war, Joel 3:9B. We're supposed to be making Earth more like Heaven. Agree with God, so you can win the war and so God will bring heavenly conditions to your life.

Prelude to Prayer

Lord, wake me up, alert me, get me up when it's time to pray. Fill me with the *spirit of prayer--*, that I pray all kinds of prayers and I'm effective in the spirit, in the Name of Jesus. Lord, if anyone is enchanting against me, hunting me, hunting my star, wake me up if I'm sleeping, get me up if I'm resting, stir me up if I'm idle, and fire me up by the Holy Spirit, in the Name of Jesus, Amen.

Love Does Not Boast

God made you; He put good things in the star that He made for you. In your dominion, in your authority you need to protect those things. If your natural dad gave you a car, wouldn't you take care of it and protect it? You are spirit, you have spiritual gifts, and you need to *spiritually* protect them. Don't run your mouth all the time and brag about what you have, what you get, what you can do. That's just drawing all the wrong kind of attention to you. Try not to do that.

Love is not boastful. We're in Christ, and Christ is **love**. We're not boastful and puffed up. There are strong, seasoned, evil star hunters, and they may just be looking for you because of your mouth.

By the time Herod was killing all the male children under the age of two years old, Jesus's parents had already gotten Him out of Dodge, they had gotten Jesus out of town, out of harm's way. People spread the word of Jesus' birth, but I'm sure Mary and Joseph weren't bragging, *"Look at our boy!"* We are warned often in Scriptures to guard our mouth.

You have to make sure that your steps are ordered by God for your life, for your protection, and also that you're in the right place where God commands the blessings for you.

Stop bragging and start praying. Start listening to God. Because stars can be stolen and caged by defilement, as I said, by eating in the dream and also by eating food dedicated to idols. Also eating *charmed* food is a way many are captured, every day in the natural world.

When you participate in pagan holidays and festivals, such as Halloween or any version of Halloween, you're agreeing with the highest day of Satan in the year. I don't know why any parent would do that, because it's not like your children don't get candy all year. And aside from razor blades and needles and all the other evil in the candy-, if people would put razor blades and needles and candy, what else do you think they're doing? What other enchantments do you think they're putting on this candy that your child is bringing home and eating? This stuff is defiled. This candy should not be brought into your home. Your child should not be eating it.

Doing so could initiate your child into something satanic. Most want to think that evil done to charm Halloween candy is a one off. *Really*? There are a **million** people in the USA alone practicing witchcraft, so only *one* person out of a million decided to do that, all on their own and no one else?

This evil candy has been polluted, weaponized and it is now going to traumatize the child in the natural who eats it. The enchantment is in there too, the programming is in there—more trauma, this time spiritual trauma. The devil loves trauma. We don't want anything to happen to your child that they get cut, hurt, or poisoned. We do not want your child enchanted, cursed, deceived, or initiated by darkness.

This is as good as evil wants it. And then dressing up for Halloween, and the carved pumpkin at the door, this initiates your child into Satan's camp. That carved pumpkin at the front door indicates to Satan that he can have your youngest.

The Doorpost

On spiritual protection, I read in the Bible that you're supposed to have the Blood of Jesus over the doorpost and the lentils of your door, not a pumpkin, not a gourd. So what are we doing? If you think it's safe to take your kid trick or treating because it's your neighborhood, or a "good" neighborhood, you may be sadly mistaken. Diviners can make plenty of money and can live in nice neighborhoods if they want to.

If you think you can discern a witch by what they *look* like, that's not discernment--, that's guesswork. A lot of people who practice the occult look like normal folk. They look like the people in your neighborhood, those at your grocery store. A lot of them look like normal folks. Many of them go to church and they can rebuke with the best of them. They can talk that talk, which doesn't make them a Christian.

So why risk your kid's health and life, and their future for a piece of candy that you can just go to the store and buy? You can *make* candy. You guys can make candy instead of celebrating the very highest (my word), *hollow day* of Satan in the year.

Why would you want to worship with the people who are celebrating that holiday with Satan? You want to teach your kid how to masquerade? *Why*? You want to teach your kid to go from door to door to beg. Why would you ever want to teach a child that they need **THAT MUCH** candy all at once? **Why**?

Extended WARFARE PRAYERS

Repentance, Renunciation, Mercy

I'm A Star

Evil Altars

Star Placement/Position

Destiny/Destiny Helpers

Star Visibility

Death

Divine Connections

Judgement

Deliverance

Restoration

Exhortation & Worship

Repentance, Renunciation, Mercy

Lord Jesus, I come to You asking for Mercy where I have failed, in Jesus' Name.

I renounce all evil covenants I've agreed to, either knowingly or unknowingly. I break every evil curse against my life. I bind every demon assigned to enforce every curse, in the Name of Jesus.

Anything in me that is blocking Heaven from fighting for me, I repent of it, in the Name of Jesus.

I plead the Blood of Jesus over my spirit, soul, and body right now, Holy Spirit help me pray, assist my prayers, in the Name of Jesus.

We need to speak the Word of God from our place of Dominion and in our God-given authority to assist our angels in their works on our behalf. God, the Earth, our country, our state, our city, our neighborhood, ourselves and our fellow man. Amen.

Father, I repent of any and every sin I personally have committed against You and Your Word, in the Name of Jesus. Lord, show me my sins that are hidden to me, so I may fully repent. Lord, please forgive me.

Lord, forgive me if I've compromised or lost my birthright star for any reason, especially by works of the flesh, in the Name of Jesus. Lord, have Mercy, hear my repentance. Cover me with the Blood of Jesus and restore my star, in the Name of Jesus.

I repent for my ancestors back 10 generations on each side of my family, for all their sins, indiscretions, evil oaths, evil vows, loyalty and blood oaths in any secret society, in the Name of Jesus.

Lord, cover us with Your Grace and Mercy, and the Blood of Jesus. Lord, I repent for sins committed by anyone from my bloodline. Anyone who has recited and enacted the Thousand Oaths, or the any evil oath required to join any secret society. Lord, I ask forgiveness if I pledged allegiance to any foreign *little g god*.

I ask the Blood of Jesus to cover these sins and wash me clean, in the Name of Jesus.

I'm A Star

Father, I am a descendant of Abraham. Count me in the multitude of Your glorious stars.

You know all the stars by name. **Lord, call my name. Lord, look on me.** Help me to do my assigned work here and fulfill destiny. All to Your glory, make me shine, help me shine in Jesus' Name.

Star of Joseph, star of my destiny, be stabilized, not wandering, Lord put Holy Ghost stability and protection around my star. Let the light of my star burn the retinas of every evil agent spying it out. Let them be blinded and be forced to look away. Leave my star alone. Lose my location, lose the location of my star, in the Name of Jesus.

Heavens, praise the Lord for which you were created. Refuse to conduct warfare against my life, in the Name of Jesus.

Daystar, arise. We have also a more sure word of prophecy, where until you do well to take heed as unto a light that shines in a dark place, until the dawn, the day dawns, and the Daystar arise in your hearts.

Let Christ arise in my heart and direct my paths, that my future is bright, that God is glorified, and I reach destiny. Amen.

Evil Altars

Any ancestral dedication of my life to idols or occultic powers, I break you now, and I cancel you by the power of the Holy Spirit, in the Name of Jesus.

I take authority over the effects of the elements, especially the *Triangular Powers*. The sun, the moon, and the stars, by commanding the day and commanding the night, in the Name of Jesus.

Every altar against me programmed into the *Triangular Powers*, lose your programming, lose your calendar, lose your clock and timer against me, and roast to ashes, by Fire and brimstone right now, in the Name of Jesus.

Any spiritual exchange over my destiny that was done in collaboration with altars of my father's house or my mother's house, be nullified and reversed now by the power in the Name of Jesus.

Ancestral powers that have swallowed my glory, be overcome with Holy Ghost nausea and vomit my glory by fire now, in the Name of Jesus.

By Thunder, by Fire, I break up every evil altar erected against me, in the Name of Jesus.

Every evil altar that has struck at my star, the Lord Jesus rebuke you, and you be struck back by the fire and the Thunder Hammer of the Holy Ghost, in Jesus' Name.

Star Placement/Position

Wandering Star, confused star, be stabilized now by the power of God, in Jesus' Name.

Cloud of Darkness over my star, roll away now by the Wind of God, in the Name of Jesus.

Any power assigned to stagnate my star, die, in the Name of Jesus.

Powers that have satanically repositioned my star die, in the Name of Jesus.

You, my star, arise and move to the right position, in the Name of Jesus. Any satanic exchange done to my star, receive deliverance, in Jesus' Name.

Angels of the Most High God, do battle for me in the heavenlies and release my star from any and all captivity, in the Name of Jesus.

You, wandering star, wherever you are, I command you to **return home**, in the Name of Jesus. Witchcraft curses targeted to make my star wander, break, in the Name of Jesus.

I bind every devil assigned to enforce any curse against me or my star, in Jesus' Name.

My star, find your right position by Fire and shine, in Jesus' Name.

Lord, arise and reposition my star for good and to Your glory, in the Name of Jesus.

Destiny/Destiny Helpers

My original destiny, appear by Fire, in the Name of Jesus.

Whatever is separating me from my divine helpers catch Fire, in the Name of Jesus.

My star, shine so my destiny helpers will find me, in Jesus' Name.

My star, shine so that divine connections can be made to the glory of God, in the Name of Jesus.

My star, shine so the favor of God and of man is upon my life, in the Name of Jesus.

Thank You, Lord, for length of days on the Earth and for my star which shines brightly to draw destiny helpers, and favor, in Jesus' Name.

Star Visibility

Darkness of my father's house, or my mother's house, you shall not cover my star, in the Name of Jesus.

Darkness of any friend's house or relative's house. In-laws, Ex's, house, former in-laws house--, people I've long forgiven and forgotten, but you're still hanging on, lurking, stalking -- you will not cover my star, in the Name of Jesus.

Oh Lord, my God, burn off every covering cast over my star and then cover my star with Holy Ghost *FIRE*, in Jesus' Name.

My star, if you are captive, Angels of God rescue my star. My star, receive deliverance now, in Jesus' Name.

Evil Star Exchanges

Heavenly Father, every door that I have opened to allow for any spiritual star exchange, forgive me, in the Name of Jesus. I close every evil door, in the Name of Jesus.

I come before You to make declarations and decrees against spiritual exchange and spiritual star exchange. Lord, reverse all evil spiritual exchange, in the Name of Jesus.

Every spiritual exchange that the enemy has done against my life, be annulled, in the Name of Jesus.

Father, any case of *Triangular Power* evil which the enemy intends to release against my life, every star tampering, star jacking, star exchange, past, present or planned for the future, be canceled and nullified, in the Name of Jesus.

Father, You said in Your Word that no one has the power to declare anything over my life that will come to pass; I declare that no spiritual exchange can take place over my star, life, and/or destiny, in the Name of Jesus.

Every spiritual pit to exchange my star, any virtue, any good thing from God, in which the enemy has dug in my name, I come with Double

Thunder and declare I shall not fall into that pit, but the enemy shall find that pit, or that pit shall find the evil agent, in the Name of Jesus.

Thank You, Lord for delivering me from evil spiritual exchanges and delivering my star from the hands of any and every enemy, in the Name of Jesus.

Every exchange of star which resulted in or from the exchange of spiritual garment in my life and destiny, CHANGE back to my original God-given garment, in Jesus Name.

Lord, any wrong garment, any evil garment that I am wearing in the spirit, I return it now, back to sender, in the Name of Jesus.

Anything the enemy has given to me, any evil thing in my possession, I return it by FIRE now, in the Name of Jesus.

Anything, especially any evil thing that the spiritual exchange of star, or garment has brought into my life, I return it immediately. Lord, all negative things that were introduced into my life by evil exchange, remove those things from my life, in the Name of Jesus. Lord, judge them in the Name of Jesus.

Heavenly Father, my life is in my star, my health, my education, my wealth, my marriage, my children, my favor, my destiny. Every sickness, poverty, oppression, disfavor, singlehood, loneliness, barrenness, or divorce which resulted from evil exchange, caging, burying, or removal of my star, I reject and fire back to senders, in the Name of Jesus.

Lord, thank You for restoration of my original garment that will now bring me joy, blessings, promotions, and glory to overshadow all sorrows, all afflictions, disappointments that I've suffered, in the Name of Jesus.

For every evil garment that I've masqueraded in, camouflaged in--, Lord, I repent. I repent of Halloween and willingly putting on evil garments, in the Name of Jesus. I repent of putting on every evil garment, in Jesus' Name.

All evil outfits, burn off by Fire, in the Name of Jesus. Father, restore me to my original garments that You have for my life. Restore my cloak of many colors. My cloak of **_any_** color as long as it's from You, Father.

Thank You, Lord.

Lord, restore my signet ring signifying who I am and *whose* I am. I'm not prodigal. I am in Jesus Christ and *all in.*

Death

Father, wherever star exchanges are coming from that would cause or try to cause death in my life or death of any good thing in my life, it is returned back to sender, in the Name of Jesus.

Every spell whether *triangulated* or not, every spell of death against me, my star, or any part of my life, be annulled by the power in the Blood of Jesus, in the Name of Jesus.

Lord, I will only depart this Earth according to Your schedule after the fulfillment of my life's assignments, in the Name of Jesus.

Any wicked personality anointed to destroy my life, destroy your own life, in the Name of Jesus.

Nothing will separate me from the Love of God that is in Christ Jesus, and nothing will cut me off before my time on Earth, in the Name of Jesus.

No spiritual exchange will terminate the breath of God in my nostrils, in Jesus' Name.

Thank You, Lord, for length of days on the Earth and for my star which shines brightly to draw destiny, destiny helpers, favor, health, education, wealth, prosperity, success, marriage, family, and children, in Jesus' Name.

Lord, anyone who has exchanged my star for theirs or anyone else's, I reject the exchange. Just as David couldn't fight in another man's armor, there is nothing I can do with another person's star. I send their star back to them and I snatch my star back by the power of the Holy Spirit, in the Name of Jesus.

Anyone who is trying to kill my star, let their star die the death they had planned for my star. Any power that is trying to kill my star, let that power die the death, in Jesus' Name.

Father every evil altar that is responsible for star exchange in my life, I command the release of Your Judgment of Fire against them, in the Name of Jesus.

All wicked hunters that plan to pursue me until I die, you're a liar--, I bind every power that is supporting or networking with you. Fall down and die, in the Name of Jesus.

Every evil archer, every shootist in the darkness, every evil archer--, **Hunters of Heaven** pursue them now and overtake them, in the Name of Jesus.

Thank You, Lord, for answering all these prayers, to You be all the glory of honor the power.

Glory killers, my life is not for experiment, collide with the Rock of Ages, in the Name of Jesus.

I will not die the death of my enemy. I will not die with my enemies, in Jesus' Name.

No soul hunter shall waste my life, in the Name of Jesus.

Powers waiting to kill me at my unguarded hour, **die** in the Name of Jesus. Lord, set a hedge of protection about me, a wall of Fire, hedge Fire, a mountain of Fire so I'm never unguarded. Lord set a guard of Mighty Angels to keep me from attack by the enemy, at every access point, in the Name of Jesus.

Any power planning to use my life as a sacrifice, I'm not your candidate; the Lord Jesus disallow it and rebuke you. Die in Jesus' Name.

Every tampering of my star to cause death of anything in my life, my education, career, profession, marriage, family, children, purpose, ministry or destiny, be reversed, in the Name of Jesus. Back to sender with a double portion.

My star will not set at the wrong time, in Jesus' Name.

Divine Connections

Father, divine connections I've missed because of star tampering, restore every opportunity to me now; redeem the time, in the Name of Jesus.

Angels of God, Holy Father, retrieve me from wrong positions, wrong places, in the spiritual and natural, in the Name of Jesus.

Lord, restore me back to my rightful position and place, in the Name of Jesus.

Father, thank You for the restoration of my original spiritual garment which you gave me, in the Name of Jesus.

Father, whoever has the authority to give me the opportunities that have been denied as a result of this evil exchange or star tampering, Lord, bring unction to that person to give me what is mine, in Jesus' Name.

Judgement

Lord, arise as a Man of War, because You are, and disgrace openly all the enemies of my destiny that don't want me to arise and shine, in the Name of Jesus.

Every dark power using *Triangular Powers* to attack me or my star, die, in the Name of Jesus.

I disconnect my life from all evil that uses *Triangular Powers,* in the Name of Jesus. Every evil arrow from the sun, moon, and stars, miss your target, you shall not strike me. Back to sender.

Father, I command judgmental Fire against every spirit, power, wickedness in high places, and every authority that has been responsible for any star tampering, star jacking, or exchange against my star, and against any of my blessings, in the Name of Jesus.

Lord, let there be multiplication of every good thing from here on out, and let me recover quickly all the enemy has taken from me, in the Name of Jesus.

Lord, reverse every spiritual exchange which the enemy has done in my life, in the Name of Jesus.

Wickedness against my star shall not prosper, in the Name of Jesus.

Blood of Jesus, destroy all inherited curses in my life, in the Name of Jesus.

Power of the scattering curse, fail woefully, you will not scatter my destiny, in the Name of Jesus. Return to sender.

I rebuke every word curse ever spoken over me from my inception to right now, in the Name of Jesus.

Lord, I repent for every negative, ungodly or unproductive thing *I* have ever said about *myself*, in the Name of Jesus. Lord, cancel every evil assignment that has resulted in any word curse spoken over me, even if I spoke it over myself.

Powers behind instability and wandering in my life, be arrested by fire, in Jesus' Name.

All satanic hunters of my father's, mother's, relatives, ex's, schoolmates, colleagues, co-workers, former co-workers, former college buddies', strangers, enemies' houses lose my location, lose my star's location. Forget my coordinates, return to senders. All unrepentant enemies of God, receive arrows of Fire, and die suddenly, in the Name of Jesus.

Lord, I cry for Mercy as I call for divine judgment on every wicked star hunter that's hunting against my star, in the Name of Jesus.

The Lord gives me the fruit of my own labor, it is not for the enemy to enjoy, in the Name of Jesus.

Father, every evil spirit, power, or principality responsible for the spiritual exchange of may star and or destiny, I call down Holy Ghost Fire on them, in the Name of Jesus.

Evil enchanter, witch, or wizard working against me, either on your own behalf or by proxy, forget my name, lose my coordinates, lose my location, in the Name of Jesus, I send you confusion from the war room of God.

Every Sorcerer or diviner assigned to terminate my destiny, be frustrated and confused; run mad, in the Name of Jesus.

I command the dark powers that have swallowed my virtues to vomit them now, in the Name of Jesus.

The problems that defeated my parents shall not defeat me, in the Name of Jesus.

Anti breakthrough powers against my life, die, in the Name of Jesus.

Satanic aggression against my star, die, in the Name of Jesus.

Powers that have vowed to cage or suffocate my star, be pulverized by the Thunder Hammer of God, in Jesus' Name.

Any enchantment of any satanic entity or human agent, backfire by Fire, in the Name of Jesus.

Every evil programmed using *Triangular Powers*, into the sun, moon and or stars against my relationships, the Lord Jesus denies you access to me. Backfire, return to sender. Let *your* relationships be dismantled and destroyed. Whatever you have planned for me, you have it, in the Name of Jesus.

Every arrow charmed with the *Triangular Powers*, release me and locate your owner--, back to sender with Holy Ghost Smoke and Holy Ghost Fire, in the Name of Jesus.

Agenda of wickedness against my life expire (X3).

Evil timetables, evil timelines, evil scrolls--, every handwriting against me, *triangulated* with the moon, sun, or stars, receive the razor of God and be shredded, and then burn to ashes, in the Name of Jesus.

Every battle in the heavenlies against my star, calling, or ministry hear the Word of the Lord, scatter by Thunder, in Jesus' Name.

Powers assigned to disgrace my destiny from Satanic headquarters, be disgraced, in Jesus' Name.

Every satanic agenda against my destiny and the heavenlies fail by Fire, in Jesus' Name.

Every power dedicated to monitoring or blocking me be paralyzed by Fire, in the Name of Jesus.

Every evil finger pointing at my star be paralyzed, wither and die, in the Name of Jesus.

Every power blocking my blessings in the 2nd heaven, be destroyed by the whirlwind of Heaven, in the Name of Jesus.

By the Thunder of God, I deafen the ears of every sorcerer or diviner listening for information regarding me or my star, in the Name of Jesus.

Every evil agent trying to direct, hijack, steal, or star jack my star, or stop my destiny, die, in the Name of Jesus.

Lord, raise up an adversary against the enemies of my destiny, in the Name of Jesus.

Angels of God chase every demon that threatens my life back to the abyss from where they cannot return, in the Name of Jesus.

Every evil person, entity, or power that is working against my life, health, success, marriage, and/or family, Lord Jesus, cut off their power from all other powers and from all the elements, in the Name of Jesus.

Every evil incantation uttered into the sun, moon, stars, water, earth, wind, fire, or any pot, charm--, anything against me be nullified by the Blood of Jesus.

Any power that has seen my God-given future and has vowed to destroy it, steal it or block it, fall down and die, in the Name of Jesus.

Powers investigating my future, receive blindness, in the Name of Jesus. I fight in the *spirit of Jehu*. Let the throne of witchcraft in my life be uprooted by Fire and blown away to desolation, by the Wind of God.

Deliverance

God arise in the Thunder of Your power and change my story to glory, in Jesus' Name.

Anything in me that is blocking God from hearing and answering my prayer come up and out, in Jesus' Name. I receive deliverance now.

Multiple witchcraft hunters hunting my star, anyone who has ever hunted my star, waste yourself, in the Name of Jesus.

Lord, set me free from every region of captivity where I've been captive by my own sins, by ancestral curse, or evil foundation, in the Name of Jesus.

Lord, remove all little g *gods* and their influences from our lives, in Jesus' Name.

Lord, open every locked prison gate, in every realm, send Your angels to free me from every captivity, in the Name of Jesus.

My star, refuse to betray me. Stop telling my secrets. Do not listen to the voice of anyone but God, God's representatives, and me, in the Name of Jesus.

Every long-awaited blessing   that belongs to me, that was hijacked by the powers in the 2nd heaven, be released by Fire, in the Name of Jesus.

Angels of my deliverance hijacked in the heavenlies, be released by Fire, in Jesus' Name.

My star, if you are captive, Angels of God rescue my star. My star receive deliverance now, in Jesus' Name.

Thank You, Lord, for Salvation and deliverance from this evil trap, in Jesus' Name.

Restoration

Restore me to Your divine favor, in the Name of Jesus.

Anything the enemy has taken from me in any age, realm, dimension, or any timeline-, past, present, and plans to take from me in the future, I ask now that the Blood of Jesus speak for me.

Any part of my destiny that has changed as a result of my star being star jacked, stolen, lost or exchanged – every evil change that has been done against my life, Father, reverse those changes, in the Name of Jesus.

Where I've been robbed and *nothing* was given to me, Lord, restore, in the Name of Jesus.

Where I've been robbed and counterfeit replacements have been given to me, Lord I send all counterfeit blessings back to sender and I reclaim what is rightfully mine, now, in the Name of Jesus.

I receive back my original destiny in You Lord. You have plans for me for a future and a prosperous end, in the Name of Jesus.

Father,   everything that I've been deprived of as a result of star jacking and/or destiny exchange, return to me, by Your Word, seven-fold. Sevenfold opportunities, favor, and privileges, in the Name of Jesus.

Father, thank You for restoration of my destiny, in the Name of Jesus.

Father, every evil priest or priestess responsible for any type of star jacking against me, and my destiny, Lord deal with them according to their own wickedness, in the Name of Jesus.

Father, I know that You are a God of restoration and I know that You can restore the *times* and *seasons* of my life which the spiritual exchange has deprived me of. I ask for speedy recovery of all the times and seasons that I have missed as a result of every spiritual exchange which the enemy has done in my life, in the Name of Jesus.

Father, whatever divine doors I have missed as a result of every spiritual exchange of the enemy against my star, I pray for the restoration of those divine doors, and that they will be open to me, in the Name of Jesus.

My original destiny, appear by Fire, in the Name of Jesus.

For every evil garment that I've masqueraded in, camouflaged in-- Lord, I repent. I repent of Halloween masquerades and willingly putting on evil garments, in the Name of Jesus. I repent of putting on every evil garment, in Jesus' Name.

All evil outfits burn off by Fire, in the Name of Jesus. Father, restore me to my original garments that You have for my life. Restore my cloak of many colors. My cloak of **_any_** color as long as it's from You, Father. Thank You, Lord.

Lord, restore my position in Christ. I'm not prodigal. I am in Jesus Christ. Thank you.

Father, I return whatever the enemy has placed in my life through evil exchange of any kind, including star exchange, or any type of tampering with my star, in the Name of Jesus.

Father, in the Name of Jesus, restore the years that the locusts, the palmer worm, the caterpillar, have eaten. Restore whatever has been taken from me personally and my family, in the Name of Jesus.

Heal me and my family, in Jesus' Name.

All that rightfully belongs to me in the heavenlies, be released unto me by Fire, in the Name of Jesus.

I recover all my goodness and virtue stolen by star hunters, in the Name of Jesus.

Protection

Angels of God, you are assigned and, on your post, to protect me from evil, in the Name of Jesus.

Spirit of retaliation, I bind you. You will not have an open door to return or pay me back, for these prayers, or for breaking **evil covenants**, in the Name of Jesus

Lord, by Your mighty angels, seal up every dimensional access point to my life, against evil interlopers, in the Name of Jesus.

Exhortation & Worship

Thank You, Lord Jesus. You are the Light of the World. You are our Salvation. You are our Peace. You are the Truth. I bless You, Lord, in the Name of Jesus, I bless You. Thank You, Lord. Amen.

I command myself, my soul, spirit, body, and my entire being to enter into the realm of my destiny in Christ Jesus. Amen.

I seal these declarations across every realm, age, timeline and dimension, past, present and future to Infinity, in the mighty Name of Jesus. Thank You, Lord. *Amen.*

Other books by this author

Already Married in the Spirit: *Why You May Not Be Married in the Natural*

AMONG SOME THIEVES

Ancestral Powers

Anti-Marriage, *The Spirit of*

Backstabbers https://a.co/d/gi8iBxf

Barrenness, *Prayers Against* https://a.co/d/feUltIs

Battlefield of Marriage, *The*

Prayers Against Beauty Curses

Beware of the Dog: Prayers Against Dogs in the Dream.

Bless Your Food: *Let the Dining Table be Undefiled*

Blindsided: *Has the Old Man Bewitched You?* https://a.co/d/5O2fLLR

Break Free from Collective Captivity

Broken Spirits & Dry Bones

Casting Down Imaginations

Churchzilla, The Wanna-Be, Supposed-to-be Bride of Christ

Demonic Cobwebs (prayerbook)

Demonic Time Bombs

Demons Hate Questions

Devil Loves Trauma, *The*

Devil Weapons: Unforgiveness, Bitterness,…

The Devourers: Thieves of Darkness 2

Do Not Swear by the Moon

Don't Refuse Me, Lord (4 book series)
https://a.co/d/idP34LG

Dream Defilement

The Emptiers: *Thieves of Darkness, 1*
https://a.co/d/5I4n5mc

Every Evil Bird (prayerbook)

Evil Touch

Failed Assignment

Fantasy Spirit Spouse https://a.co/d/hW7oYbX

FAT Demons (The): *Breaking Demonic Curses*
https://a.co/d/4kP8wV1

The Fold (5-book series)

My Sowing Journal

Gang Ups: Touch Not God's Anointed

Getting Rid of Evil Spiritual Food
https://a.co/d/i2L3WYQ

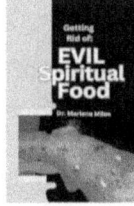

got HEALING? Verses for Life

got LOVE? Verses for Life

got HOPE? Verses for Life

got money? https://a.co/d/g2av41N

How to Dental Assist

How to Dental Assist2: Be Productive, Not Wasteful

How to STOP Being a Blind Witch or Warlock

I Take It Back

Legacy

Let Me Have A Dollar's Worth
https://a.co/d/h8F8XgE

Level the Playing Field

Living for the NOW of God

Lose My Location https://a.co/d/crD6mV9

Love Breaks Your Heart

Made Perfect In Love

Mammon

Man Safari, *The*

Marriage Ed. Rules of Engagement & Marriage

Made Perfect in Love

Money Hunters: Beware of Those

Money on the Altar https://a.co/d/4EqJ2Nr

Mulberry Tree, *The* https://a.co/d/9nR9rRb

Motherboard (The) - *Soul Prosperity Series*

Name Your Seed

Occupy: *Until I Return*

Plantation Souls

Players Gonna Play

Power Money: Nine Times the Tithe
https://a.co/d/gRt41gy

The Power of Wealth *(forthcoming)*

Powers Above

The Robe, Part 1, The Lessons of Joseph

The Robe, Part II, The Lessons of Joseph

Seasons of Grief

Seasons of Waiting

Seasons of War

Second Marriage, Third--, *Any Marriage*
https://a.co/d/6m6GN4N

Sift You Like Wheat

Six Men Short: What Has Happened to all the Men?

Soul Prosperity soul prosperity series 3

https://a.co/d/5p8YvCN

Souls Captivity soul prosperity series 2

The Spirit of Anti-Marriage

The Spirit of Poverty

StarStruck

SUNBLOCK

The Swallowers: *Thieves of Darkness*, 3

Take It Back

This Is NOT That: *How to Keep Demons from Coming at You*

Time Is of the Essence

Too Many Wives: *Why You Have Lady Problems*

Tormenting Spirits   https://a.co/d/dAogEJf

Toxic Souls

Triangular Power *(series)*

Unbreak My Heart: *Don't Let Me Die*

Uncontested Doom

Unguarded Hours, *The*

Unseen Life, *The* (forthcoming)

Upgrade: How to Get Out of Survival Mode

- Toxic Souls (Book 2 of series)
- Legacy (Book 3 of series)

The Wasters: *Thieves of Darkness*, Bk 2
https://a.co/d/bUvI9Jo

What Have You to Declare? What Do You Have With You from Where You've Been?

When the Devourer is Rebuked

https://a.co/d/1HVv8oq

The Wilderness Romance *(series)* This series is about conducting a Godly relationship and marriage with someone who is a Wilderness person. It is about how to recognize it and navigate through it. These books are about how not to get caught up in such.

- *The Social Wilderness*
- *The Sexual Wilderness*
- *The Spiritual Wilderness*

Other Series

Soul Prosperity Series
https://a.co/d/bz2M42q

Spirit Spouse books

https://a.co/d/9VehDSo

https://a.co/d/97sKOwm

Battlefield of Marriage, The
https://a.co/d/eUDzizO

Players Gonna Play https://a.co/d/2hzGw3N

Matters of the Heart (series)

Made Perfect in Love https://a.co/d/70MQW3O

Love Breaks Your Heart https://a.co/d/4KvuQLZ

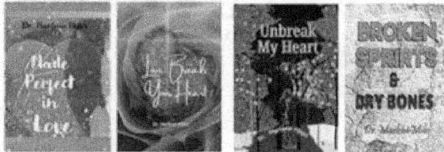

Unbreak My Heart
https://a.co/d/84ceZ6M

Broken Spirits & Dry Bones
https://a.co/d/e6iedNP

Thieves of Darkness series

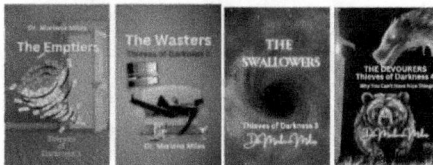

The Emptiers https://a.co/d/heio0dO

The Wasters https://a.co/d/5TG1iNQ

The Swallowers https://a.co/d/1jWhM6G

The Devourers: Why We Can't Have Nice Things
https://a.co/d/87Tejbf

Triangular Powers
https://a.co/d/aUCjAWC

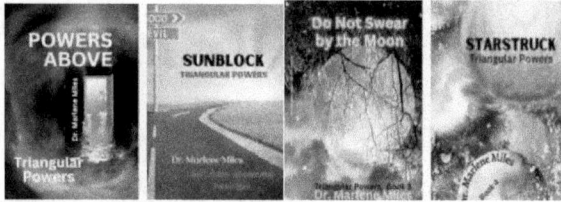

Upgrade (series) *How to Get Out of Survival Mode* https://a.co/d/aTERhXO